The Double Mind

An Expository and Devotional Study
From The Epistle of James

by

Don J. Kenyon, Th.M.

Christian Publications, Inc.
Harrisburg, Pennsylvania

Reprinted 1980
by
Christian Publications, Inc., from the
1959 edition issued by Zondervan
Publishing House.
© 1959 by Don J. Kenyon

The mark of *OP* vibrant faith

Christian Publications, Inc.
25 S. 10th Street, P.O. Box 3404
Harrisburg, PA 17105
ISBN: 0-87509-288-8
Library of Congress Catalog Card No. 80-68255
Printed in the United States of America

Contents

Preface

This book is the evolution of a conviction. The name which it bears is not original. This term was used by James, the brother of Jesus, to describe a nation's spiritual condition after two thousand years of religious heritage. The same term—double-minded—cannot be improved on in describing the Church of Jesus Christ after almost two more millenniums of background. It is the intention of the author that this volume be provocative—certainly not exhaustive. It is deliberately brief. It should be read, if possible, at one sitting. Much of the body of the material is in the language of the lay-reader. Therefore the footnotes are designed to lead the interested student of the Word into the text of the Bible to discover for himself the basis for some of the statements which are made.

The general content grew out of a series of studies on the Epistle of James delivered from time to time in churches, Bible conferences and the classroom. Many requests for "notes" or copies of these studies have led to the preparation of the general outline of the lessons in book form.

This book is meant to be helpful, not critical. Truth usually speaks for itself without too much human embellishment. It is felt that the message herein will help many honest Christians see why they are barren and ineffective.

I am deeply indebted to my wife for long hours spent with me in patient criticism and suggestions, and to others who have read the manuscript and corrected the text.

Don J. Kenyon

Introduction

When James wrote his epistle to his beloved brethren, he was probably the first Christian to take up the pen in defense of the Church. Judaism was sterile. The Church at Jerusalem was choked by tradition and prejudice. It had virtually become ingrown. There were few if any so well qualified as James to cry against the situation. His position of honored leadership did not blind him to the problems he faced in Judah's "eternal city." His spirit had been saturated with the teaching of Christ whose servant he had now become. His loyalty had been pledged to his nation. This loyalty was staunchly maintained though he died a martyr because it was misunderstood. Although some of Judah's zealous patriots preferred to show their devotion to the dying nation by shedding their blood while holding back the enraged armies of Rome, James chose a more practical and enduring way to serve. The very nature of his message has made it the most misunderstood and neglected portion of the New Testament canon. The fact that it was directed—in language that favors old covenant terminology and style—to a nation that had "stumbled at the stumblingstone" of a crucified Messiah has certainly not been in its favor. The Epistle of James has, however, been coming into its own lately. Many fine volumes have been published which do justice to its vital message. Our age with its warped idea of Christian morality has made it necessary for the trumpet of ethical truth to be sounded again and again, and with no uncertain sound.

Basic ethics are timeless. It has been the overemphasis upon the gracious aspect of redemption that has given many sincere Christians the erroneous idea that the "standard of grace" is essentially a license to lawlessness. God be thanked that we are no longer "under law," but this cannot be construed by a generation already tragically loose in its morals to mean "without law to Christ."

To see James deal with legally minded people who were having the inward conflict so vividly described by Paul in Romans 7 is a great spiritual adventure—if one delves deeply enough into the message of James to apprehend it. Whereas Paul approaches the subject by defining the nature and function of the Law, James deals with the spirit of the Law. Paul resolves the conflict by showing that the Law was never intended to be our savior. James shows that Christ gives a man, through the power of the indwelling Spirit, the dynamic to fulfill the righteousness of the Law. To both Paul and James the life and walk in the Spirit was equivalent to manifesting the nature of God who through Christ saved us by His death and resurrection. With Paul faith was active and virile (Rom. 4:20-25). With James an active and virile life was the evidence of faith. Paul was looking at the dynamic. James looked for the evidences of that dynamic.

This book takes the rather unpopular viewpoint of James that without the effects of ethical energy in the Holy Spirit, a faith which does not manifest itself in God-ordained works is as convincing as a corpse. We have seen a theological miracle performed in our age. We have managed somehow to turn the wine of holy living back into the water of moral laxity and have done so in the name of Christ who died to reverse the order. Thus the message of James is addressed to a condition of heart—double-mindedness—which refuses to be confined to dispensational boundaries.

1

The Lion Roars

Will a lion roar in the forest,
when he hath no prey?
                    —Amos 3:4

James, the brother of our Lord, and the eldest of the sons of Joseph and Mary,[1] was specially[2] commissioned by the resurrected Christ to a position of grave and delicate responsibility. To lead the loosely organized church through its earliest stages[3] of growth and development before the hub of its activity shifted from Judea to Syria, was no small assignment. This patient, adamant man sealed his loyalty to the Lord as one of the earliest martyrs, stoned by "his beloved brethren" at the order of a pettish procurator.[4]

His life might be called "the triumph of the transition." Before Christianity shifted its emphasis to the Gospel of God as revealed to the Apostle Paul, James delivered to the ages one of its most valuable treatises on human behavior. It was written with a pen dipped in the ink of indignation. This epistle might be called an expose' of the double mind, unparalleled as an analysis of human duplicity in the sphere of religion. It ranks

James among the great prophets of denunciation—
Amos, Micah, Jeremiah—whose fearless judgments caused idolatrous Israel to tremble. Our present moral dilemma has buried this message of simplicity and clarity beneath the debris of dispensational division. For those on the fringe of victory, it is too embarrassingly practical. The exercise of spiritual discernment and an aptness to decry evil do not combine to produce a popular prophet. If one will risk being wounded by this roaring lion of ancient Jerusalem he may learn why man's religious purposes lack stability. Whereas Hosea found Judah's goodness as transient as a morning cloud,[5] James saw among his double-minded brethren a duplicity of character which caused him to liken them to a surge of the sea "driven with the wind and tossed."[6]

It is apparent in the Scripture that James held a place of esteem among a people of violent views, unbridled passions and, incongruously enough, great religious fervor. These traits combine to portray a dangerous forest in which this lion goes out to stalk his prey; one in which the hunter himself may become the hunted one. The delicate nature of his crusade for the spirit of the ancient Law of God called forth from him those qualities which he possessed naturally.

To a man schooled in the threadbare terminology of current orthodoxy James's old covenant vocabulary may seem deceivingly archaic. However the reader must bear in mind that this is transition language. It falls into the period between the Christianity of a cautious Judaistic congregation and that of a Gentile Church spreading like a prairie fire. James knew well the Lord of Hosts.[7] He knew the timeless ethics of the Decalogue. He had sensed the holy fury of the prophets. What is more important, he had learned the flavor of true wisdom from Israel's poets. We do him a grave injustice if we fail to see that he thought and wrote in an Old Testament frame of reference. His awareness of the glory and righteousness of the Ancient of Days had developed in him a true piety. This priceless quality had become intensified by a revelation of the Messiah of whom he was now a slave.[8]

This new perspective of God's holy purpose in His Son caused him to be even more sensitive to the religious inconsistencies of his brethren. One can detect James's indignation sweeping through his entire epistle. Was he not well aware of the intellectual confusion and spiritual conflict involved in turning from sterile Judaism to Christ? Had he not been a double-minded man himself as he observed his brother Jesus in those momentous days of His flesh?[9] The conflicting emotions of love for his nation, zeal for his God, hatred for injustice and hypocrisy, account for his extremes.

How in this epistle of violent conflict can he call the same people "my beloved brethren"[10] and "adulteresses"?[11] Perhaps in the same manner in which Jeremiah could weep for Jerusalem while he exposed the deep-dyed corruption which was destroying her. Modern preachers have largely lost this ability. They perhaps regard it as an inconsistency. However this is *love* in its purest form. It is the love that Christ Himself manifested at the gates of Jerusalem.

There could have been no man in Judah better qualified to help his brethren than this man who had struggled through the slough of despond into peace with God. Perhaps that is the reason the Lord of Harvest commissioned this stern lover of his nation to roar as a lion again in Judah.

---

1. Matthew 13:55. The order of the names favors this.
2. I Corinthians 15:7. The special appearance was probably for the purpose of a commission.
3. Many scholars agree that James may have been the first N. T. book.
4. The Procurator Albinus. See Josephus, *Antiquities*, Book XX, Ch. IX, 1.
5. Hosea 13:3.
6. James 1:6.
7. James 5:4.
8. James 1:1; Greek, *doulos*.
9. Cf. Mark 3:21 and 31.
10. James 1:16.
11. James 4:4. The word "adulterers" does not appear in the best manuscripts.

2

The One with Whom
We Have to Do

*All things are naked and open
unto the eyes of him with
whom we have to do.*
—Hebrews 4:13

Constancy and fervency are indispensable to prophecy. Constancy arises from a knowledge that the oracle is the Word of God. Fervency issues out of moral necessity. The true prophet must know God as He is. He must see his people as they *are*. The inquietude of spirit which these two factors may arouse in the prophet are the price of maintaining God's good pleasure. God has little comfort for the messenger whose human nature rebels in keeping these traits in proper balance.[1] He has only contempt for the false prophet who loses either or both.[2] It takes a courageous man to know the God of revelation and represent Him as He is to a wicked and perverse generation. But such a man was James the Just.

He was eaten up with zeal for the purposes of God in redemption through Christ. He sees that the salvation of his people rests in their fulfilling practically the righteousness of the ancient law of God in Christ.[3] He looks beyond the racial patriot-

14

ism which threatens to bring Rome to the gates of Jerusalem.[4] He sees the power for personal purity which can purge his people from unholy nationalism and relate them again to God's eternal purpose. His association with Christ before and after the miracle of Pentecost had caused the shuffled tenets of his traditional theology to fall into a harmony of doctrine and life. It may be said that the practicality and common sense of his message had as its fountainhead the character of its Divine Author. God was not to James a vague and fearsome figure who had projected the shadow of His glory across a corner of his life in some awesome moment in the Temple. He was now One to whom his brethren might draw near but only if they cleansed their hands and purged themselves of their double-mindedness.[5]

Precisely how is this New Covenant prophet going to get to the heart of the matter with his brethren? Some of them are floundering in a sea of religious flotsam, grasping desperately for something that will hold them up. Others of them are falling too enthusiastically into the groove of professionalism which strangles the testimony of true Christianity. Still others are piously mouthing proper Messianic formulas, but inwardly the Spirit is inoperative. To James this is vain religion.[6] With the words of Christ burning in his heart he sets about to make the tree good and its

fruit good or the tree evil and its fruit evil. He
knows well that a tree is known by its fruit. We
have with our precise theology forgotten it. But
the sharp eye of this guileless man sees instability and worldliness everywhere about him.[7] From
the sacred desk of the Christian assembly he sees
partiality and prejudice.[8] Walking the streets of
Jerusalem he observes selfishness and piosity
manifested in the midst of human misery.[9] He sees
men who have lately raised their voices in public
prayer leave the assembly and hurl invectives at
their brothers.[10] He recoils at religionists who pay
homage to moneyed men who fleece them in
business and blaspheme their Lord.[11] He marvels
at men who carry on shrewd, long-range business
speculations in utter disregard of the providence
of God.[12] How can he tolerate them? The question
is rather, how can he help them? Though a man of
God must wound, he must represent a God who
can heal. Only in this way can he speak for a God
whose wrath is against sin, yet who loves the
sinner with an everlasting love.

From this point this book deals with James's
approach to the problem of the double mind. While
it will be discussed in the setting of his epistle, a
serious endeavor will be made to identify it with
the evidences of this disease so prevalent in the
Church today. The writer's motive as previously
stated is to be helpful, not hypercritical. If the

spirit of James is maintained such will be the case.

The Bible becomes to the devout seeker after truth a Book in which God reveals His holiness as well as resolutely revealing the nature of man. The further we get from a biblical concept of God the more pridefully optimistic we become about man's inherent goodness. The more clearly we see the God of revelation the more honestly we can appraise our own depravity. Any man who looks upon the Cross of Christ as the central event of human history looks upon himself as the chiefest of sinners, guilty of nailing Him there. Since the Epistle of James was probably one of the last attempts to avert the moral suicide of a nation, it could be no passionless prophecy. The demand was for drastic measures. Judah must again see God as the One before whom all things are naked and laid open. God needed a new Ezekiel to dig into the wall of Judah's hypocrisy and expose the abominations of her secret corruption.[13] It is significant that he, James, knew *where* and *how* to begin. This, if nothing else, gives the epistle the stamp of its Holy Author. Judah must once again see her recalcitrant religion against the blazing backdrop of a revealed God. Deity must again be enthroned in the sanctuary of her mind and loved again with her whole heart. To get at the core of a prophetic denunciation one must go beyond what is said, to discover *why* it was said, and precisely why it was said *as* it was said. The student of divine revelation must seek for the God of revelation as He shows His face.

In his keynote address (1:1-18), James makes his frontal attack on the double mind by presenting three elements of God's nature which show the One with whom we have to do.

1. The Giving God

The first of these revelations (none of which is new but all of which are related contextually with new force) is to be found in 1:5. "Let him ask of God, that giveth to all men liberally." The original text states this in a manner which vividly characterizes God as the giving God.[14] This is forcibly reemphasized in 1:17 where God is called the Father of Lights who imparts all good gifts and who is the Author of all good giving.

This double emphasis on the benevolence of God is a deliberate device on the part of James to silence the spiritually impoverished and morally barren. When a man does not possess what God grants without partiality and without complexity, it is not God's deficiency. If a man knocks at the door of heaven with impudent persistence and divisive motives and does not receive, it cannot be claimed that God is reluctant to give. The man is hemmed in by the illogic of his own claim. God is a

18

gracious Giver. If we make Him to be a disinterested, far-off Sovereign—the God of deism—"we lie and do not the truth."

Here James is contending for the doctrine of his Lord and Savior ". . .it shall be *opened*. . .ye shall *find*. . .it shall be *given* you."[15] Here the inner frame of the double mind shows beneath the skin of vain religion.

2. The Guileless God

The second of these revelations is found in 1:13, "God cannot be tempted with evil." If there were any of the perfections of God of which His people had been made aware with a costly awareness, it was the oneness and holiness of Jehovah. Seventy arduous years a captive people in a pagan nation had thoroughly purged Judah from her besetting sin of idolatry.[16] This expression in 1:13 loses some of its force in the English rendition. It could be stated thus: "For God is untried with reference to evil."[17] Man reaches his lowest spiritual level when he begins to charge God with folly. It is possible in the extreme heat of trial to allow questions about God's benevolence to crowd into the heart which is already at the breaking point. But to develop a spirit of complaint toward God as a chronic attitude is indicative of a diseased religion. God is neither tempted nor does He tempt. It will be noted later where the problem lies. It is enough to say at this point that James reminds his brethren that the problem of spiritual defeat does not begin with God. It does not even begin with the rigors of life or with the nature of one's environment. If we are overcome by temptation and if sin too easily finds its mature expression in us, we must look for the cause within ourselves.[18] The moral government of the universe is just. Righteousness is the pillar which undergirds the dwelling place of God. We cannot excuse our defeat by accusing God of aiding the enemy. The history of redemption is a glorious account of victory upon victory won because Jehovah of Hosts fought for and in His own. This reiteration of the guilelessness of God prohibits the suggestion that He has brought about the circumstances from which their double-mindedness issues.

3. The Changeless God

The third revelation of this One with whom we have to do is found in the last clause of 1:17, "with whom is no variableness nor shadow of turning." Since man dwells in the atmosphere of continuous mutability there is always the danger of perverting his thoughts of God into adjustment with his changing world.

Immutability, to our thinking, is the most transcendent of God's attributes. Malachi prophesied against the chameleon charlatans of his day who went about encouraging men to social inequities and moral perversions in the name of a changeless Jehovah.[19] Age after age man attempts to alter God's laws to conform to the low level of his conduct, but God keeps reminding him through His prophets that all puny efforts to find religious respectability in theological mutations will not succeed in changing *Him*. Jeremiah chided Judah for seeking solace in a substitute.[20] One must deny the true character of the changeless God if he is to drink from the muddy puddles of yesterday's religion while professing to serve a God who is the fountain of living water. Thus Jeremiah reflected upon the tragic consequences suffered by a nation which looked with unfeigned hypocrisy to a national alliance with Egypt as a solution to her problem—a problem which rose from a traitorous abandonment of the God who had preserved her to that hour.

The double mind[21] is not a condition that can be fully isolated or pinpointed. It appears at its worst in the light of the character of the benevolent, holy and changeless God. We may observe it in this day in the utter degeneracy of apostate people who live in comfortable security while they are spiritually barren, and impudently dare God to do anything about it. The double mind is the masterpiece of Satan because it gives orthodox consent to the immutability of God while turning His grace into lasciviousness and denying His lordship. The divine logic of Scripture denies that it is possible to give consent to the doctrine of a changeless God who is conforming us to the image of His Son while at the same time we are attempting to conform Him to our own image. It is an effrontery to a holy God to smugly assign such conformity to the image of His Son to a predestined positional relationship (which it *is*) without submitting ourselves to the transformation which proves the good, and acceptable, and perfect will of God. Certainly James thought so!

----

1. Jeremiah 20:7.
2. Jeremiah 23:1, 2.
3. James 2:8-13.
4. James 5:5.
5. James 4:8.
6. James 1:26.
7. James 4:4.
8. James 2:2 ff.
9. James 2:15, 16.
10. James 3:10.
11. James 2:6, 7.
12. James 4:13, 14.
13. Ezekiel 8:7-9.
14. Let him ask, *para tou didontos theou*. Here the participle is used in its pure adjectival function characterizing God as a "giving God" thus emphasizing the *nature* of God.
15. Matthew 7:7 (italics added).
16. There is no reference to a lapse back into open idolatry among the Jews of the restoration. Interbiblical literature

to the contrary abounds with accounts of heroic resistance to any threat to her loyalty to Jehovah.

17. *ho gar theos apeirastos estin kakōn.* Literally, "For God is without experience of evil." Again note that it is a reference to the nature of God—His holiness—which is emphasized.

18. James 1:14.

19. Malachi 3:5, 6.

20. Jeremiah 2:13.

21. From *dipsuchos.* The actual meaning of the word cannot be derived so much from its etymology as from its usage. Literally, it means two-souled, from *dis and psuchē.* The man possessed of a double mind is thus a man with divided affections, divided objectives, divided judgments. This apparent use of the term need only be related to the context in which James describes his brother, to get the implicit meaning.

3

The Divine Direction

For as the new heavens and the new earth, which I will make, shall remain before me . . .so shall your. . .name remain.

—Isaiah 66:22

That the direction in which God moves in redemption is settled by His own decree is certainly not a new fact in the thinking of theologians. It is, however, a "missing link" in the reasoning of men in the school of discipline. It is a necessary premise for consistent thinking to concede that God knows where He is going in the development of His eternal purpose in Christ. No intelligent man in stressing human freedom would go so far as to take the initiative of redemption out of God's hands and put it into the hands of careless man. Since human will is the implement of man's discipline over his own behavior, the double mind strongly asserts itself in neglecting or deliberately resisting the will of God. Thus it is not surprising to see James's emphasis on God's redemptive will in the thematic passage (1:1-18). To James, the servant of the Lord Jesus Christ, the Messiah is the Jehovah of the Old Testament fulfilling His will in those who submit themselves to Him.[1]

By focusing our attention on three statements in the epistle, God's redemptive direction is seen as a unit of thought.

The Redemptive Objectives of God

1. The first of these objectives is stated in the form of a purpose clause which sets forth the ground of appeal in the exhortation of 1:2-4. This strange paradox of comfort may be stated thus: "And let patience have her perfect work, *that* you may be perfect and entire, wanting nothing."[2] The attention at this point is drawn to the end rather than the means. Whatever the process by which man arrives at God's end in view, it is clear that God's objective in redemption is to make him wholly mature inwardly. The words "perfect" and "entire" express two different elements of the same objective. Perfect, derived from the Greek word *telos*, speaks of a fulfillment, a completeness. It suggests that the thing or person made complete has reached the end intended by the perfecter. It is certain that such an objective cannot be achieved in a moment or within any specific or prescribed period. Because God is dealing with moral character it is logical that character development is essential in effecting such an end. Regeneration may make one a new creation in Christ but God's highest will is that this new creation

shall consummate in holy character. Since God is able by virtue of His power to use any means He may choose to reach this end, it may be concluded that the means He has chosen is in keeping with His master plan. With God, the Bible reveals, character is of the greatest importance. Inward growth has more abiding value to Him (and to us) than a pre-maturing deliverance. Thus it may be concluded that the objective of God is to realize a full development of the heart and mind to the point of soundness which reflects the spiritual unity of the man who is in harmony with His will.

The word "entire" further enforces this point of view. It means literally, "a full allotment."[3] Not only does this mean to be spiritually intact but in possession of all that God promises His saints in redemption. He desires that our eyes be fully opened that we may realize His inheritance in the saints. What a forceful way to call to the attention of a double-minded people that there remained for them an unclaimed inheritance! Were they to experience another national debacle because they failed to abandon a double-minded attitude?

2.   The second of these redemptive objectives forms the ground upon which James delivers a beautiful beatitude (1:12). Something vital is lost in favor of a smooth translation. The full force seems more apparent in leaving it entirely un-altered: "Blessed is the man who is enduring test-

ings, because having become approved, he shall receive the crown of life which the Lord has promised to them that love Him." Herein the blessing lies fully in the *end* which God has in view for the tested one. The aorist participle, "*having become* approved," indicates that the individual who is pronounced genuine in the crucible of fire receives the crown of life because he has demonstrated his love for God. Pushed to its ultimate logic every test of life is an occasion to prove whether we love God more or less than someone or something. This is the heart of God's desire for His people. When God sent Moses to instruct a new generation in the Law, He made it clear to them that they were to become a nation of teachers.[4] The truth which God was to grant to them was to be transmitted carefully from father to son, son to grandson, etc. It was the very life principle of the nation as well as the abiding key to her material prosperity. There was never a nation made more aware that her well-being was related to her well-doing than Israel.[5] She would rise or fall according to her devotion to her teaching mission. Immediately following the declaration of this solemn principle God reminded His elect nation that the motive of her devotion to the truth of redemption and her conduct toward Him should be *love*.[6] This love must issue out of a whole heart, a whole soul, and a whole strength. It must be so consuming that it would have preeminence in every aspect of their lives. An elect people had one duty—to demonstrate its love for the God who had chosen it. Such devotion would protect it from being overcome by Canaanitish paganism. Once again God's jealousy was emphasized by a threat of destruction.[7] This stern lesson is repeatedly brought to the attention of the wayward people by a longsuffering God and His patient messengers during the prophetic period. In short, God was not calling His people to be a nation of professional theologians. He desired above all that they should live out their love for Him. Is it not significant that it is *this* theme which was emphasized by the Son of God in His earthly ministry,[8] by Paul in dealing with Corinthian carnality;[9] and by the transcendent Lord of the Churches in exposing Ephesian laxity?[10]

3. It is the third of these objectives which should be thoughtfully pondered as the climax of God's purpose in His people. Since God wants our whole love and because He is jealous of all other lovers, it is better understood why this should be the climactic objective. It is stated in the form of a purpose clause. "Of his own will begat he us with the word of truth, *that we should be* a kind of first-fruits of his creatures" (1:18). Once again old covenant imagery may obscure the issue. Although this verse has been the ground of difference of

opinion, several things are beyond controversy. The begetting which James mentions has a specific purpose in the will of God who has thus acted. To consign this to the general creation of mankind would seem to ignore all that James has had to say up to this point. His intent is stated in an idiom of purpose relating the end in view to the act of begetting. Since the end in view is, without controversy, *redemptive,* it is only logical that a special generation for a special harvest is intended. If the seed sown is the "incorruptible seed" of God in truth, the harvest must be commensurate with the seed sown. For the purposes under discussion it would be well to examine the meaning of "firstfruits."[11] A harvest is always an indication of the seed which was planted and the care which it has had in its development and maturity. James asks: "Can a fig-tree, my brethren, yield olives, or a vine figs?" The simple law of cause and effect suffices here. If this harvest is the result of a God whose gifts are good and perfect, the result of the activity of a redemptive God, then James's purpose in this statement is to direct the mind of the reader toward God as the source of the harvest. James is adopting a figure used by Christ to cause his brethren to face again the issue of the fruit-bearing branch. The divine Husbandman is looking for fruit. This figure was embarrassingly familiar to their ears. God wants to realize something which is in keeping with His new creation in the Lord Jesus Christ. Saints under the New Covenant should by all tokens be the best of the harvest of a redemptive God. It is our vital union with His Son which is the life-giving element in producing such fruit. The Old Testament figure of first fruits does not hide the New Testament application. Many professed Christians stand today without excuse at the same level of moral barrenness which characterized Israel at the first advent. The tragedy is implicit in the fact that Calvary and Pentecost should have made a difference.

God's ultimate objective, the creation of a "new heavens and a new earth wherein dwelleth righteousness," requires a personal re-creation as well as a workmanship maturing under the wise and patient husbandry of God, manifesting itself in Spirit-motivated works which God has before ordained for the Christian's walk. Any "life" less than this is unworthy of the Creator.

---

1. James 1:18.
2. James 1:4 (italics added). The construction is *hina* with the subjunctive.
3. From *holos* meaning whole, and *Kleros* meaning lot. Our whole allotment in our Christian heritage.
4. Deuteronomy 6:7.
5. Deuteronomy 6:2, 3.
6. Deuteronomy 6:4 ff.

7. Deuteronomy 6:15, 24.
8. Matthew 5:43-48.
9. 1 Corinthians 13:1—14:1a.
10. Revelation 2:4.
11. From *aparchē*. The meaning must contextually be shaded in favor of the Old Testament. This offering was not only the first of the harvest but also the best of the harvest since it was to be offered to *God*.

The Cry for Wisdom

Doth not wisdom cry?
        —Proverbs 8:1
*That I may cause those that
love me ₍wisdom₎ to inherit
substance.*
                —Proverbs 8:21

The double mind is understood only as it is related to the key word of the epistle—*wisdom.* James introduces the idea of the double mind in an admonition to a man who would seek wisdom from God. Admission of the lack of wisdom is that which drives the man to prayer. The more keenly the lack is felt, the more persistently he ought to pray.

Once again it is the old covenant vocabulary of James that makes it necessary to define the term. What is this lack of wisdom which causes a man to seek the face of the giving God? Most scholars of the Word agree that James wrote this letter in a period in which there was little if any terminology which was distinctly "New Testament." Had he been writing to Greeks his term "wisdom" would have immediately been related to sophistry, philosophy, or worldly logic. To the Jew, however, wisdom meant one thing. Had it not been the theme of a great portion of their holy writings—

Job, Psalms, Proverbs, Ecclesiastes, Song of Solomon? In these wisdom is used without too much variation in meaning. It was familiar to the Jew and pregnant with implication. That James has the connotation of the wisdom literature of Israel in mind is borne out by his choice of this same word in his own "wisdom" passage (3:13-18).

What Is Wisdom?

The passage in James 3:13-18 begins with a question conceived in holy derision and asked with probing frankness. "Who is a wise man and endued with knowledge among you?" The word wise (*sophos*), here denotes the habit or quality of worldly "know-how"; the latter word, "understanding" (*epistēmōn*), which in the King James Version is rendered "endued with knowledge," denotes the specialized development of this quality in some particular skill. Modern terminology would have used the words "intellectual" and "expert." The question is thus addressed to the man who professes wisdom in the same hypothetical assumption as the professor of religion in 1:26 or the professor of faith in 2:14. This triad of professors claimed a quality in each case which was not validated by fact. With James a virtue professed must be a virtue manifested or it is nonexistent. Thus in his unnerving way he asks for proof.

The question is followed by a description of the wisdom which comes down from the giving God. It is contrasted with that which is earthly, sensual, devilish. By placing the *effect* before the cause James clearly points up the problem. Within the assembly were bitter jealousy, strife, and confusion. To deny these would be a deliberate falsification. Wisdom such as *this* (note well the relation of the term to actual conduct) does not descend from above. But it is standard equipment in the man who has not been liberated by the emancipating Christ. One need only follow his own senses, obey his own passions, and submit to the suggestions of the Adversary to operate in the sphere of worldly wisdom. In sharp contrast with this James describes the wisdom that God grants, in response to our admission of lack (1:5), as coming from above with all the loveliness of a heavenly impartation (3:17). As David and Solomon taught the elect nation that wisdom *was* ethical conduct in harmony with the nature of the God who chose them, so James finds it necessary once again to stress this fact. It is therefore an acknowledgment of *ethical instability* which causes the man to seek the giving God for wisdom.

In summarizing James's treatment of the subject of wisdom it is to be noted that he uses *sophia*, "wisdom," rather than *sophos* or *epistēmōn* when relating the term to the heavenly impartation.[1] And we may conclude that he is referring to the idea of practical knowledge, to truth as applied to actual life situations. Such wisdom results in a Christ-conformed person. This wisdom is a heavenly gift flowing from the ethical energy generated by the Spirit of God, showing itself in the Christian behavior of the recipient. True wisdom then, to be explicit, comes only from *God*. A man praying for wisdom is asking for more than mere mental illumination. He is conditioning his soul for that which the divine Potter will make him—i.e. the workmanship of God. An apprehension of this simple fact is necessary to understand the message of James's epistle.

It is here that double-mindedness meets its gravest test. It discovers that God imparts His wisdom in *His* way in keeping with His own nature and His own objectives in redemption. God will not bargain or quibble with men. He is a giver, impartial and gracious. He is also holy and changeless. It is we who are to be conformed to the image of His Son. It is we who are to be metamorphosed by "the renewing" of our minds (Rom. 12:2).

Let it then be understood that the double-minded man is a praying man. He is a man aware of the value of divine favor. His religion has become to him a necessary element in life. He is seeking wisdom from God in recognition of the eternal benefit which it holds for him. Were he seeking this wisdom with his whole heart he would be single-minded toward God. Were he neglecting to seek it he would be single-minded toward the world. To pray for it yet not seek it with the *whole heart* presents the problem under consideration.

---

1. James 3:17.

5

As Many as I Love

*As many as I love, I rebuke
and chasten.*
— Revelation 3:19

The philosophy of Christian maturity as set forth
by James is arduous and rugged. To adopt it one
must be a strong believer in the benevolence of
God. To grasp it requires faith and to practice it
requires holy perseverance. Many Christians may
regard it as a lofty and impractical idealism.
Indeed, to the natural mind it is "foolishness." Yet
the major problem of Christian education is to
convince the disciple of Christ that it is valid. We
live in a quasi-religious world of theological mu-
tation where our views rest largely on semantics
rather than historically stabilized biblical
exegesis. Any point of view that ripples the placid
waters of our established pattern for getting to
heaven is apt to be summarily dismissed without
sober reflection. It should then be repeated,
James's philosophy of Christian maturity is
arduous, demanding. Furthermore it is in
harmony with the time-honored procedure which
God ordained and has used in His dealings with

men since Job uttered his ancient complaint against the chastening rod of the Almighty. It is when we seek God for wisdom that we discover the extremes to which God may have to take us in order to bring us to a single-minded acceptance of this procedure.

Although it has been pointed out that wisdom is actually ethical and moral character granted graciously by God, it is the method *by which* it is granted which ferrets out the double mind. Were it possible to grant Christian maturity otherwise the double mind would never be exposed. Pretense to fervency and zeal for God will be unmasked as pure hypocrisy if they burn out at the revelation of the narrow path which leads to the watercourses of God. Thus the understanding of the double mind not only entails a comprehension of divine wisdom, the gift that is *sought*, but a comprehension of the doctrine of Christian maturity by which wisdom is *attained*. God's eternal decree not only embraces the end in view—the creation of a new heaven and a new earth wherein dwelleth righteousness, but also the process necessary to make His redeemed creatures morally righteous. Although the blessedness of positional justification in Christ cannot be minimized, the potential for the sanctification of the justified one should be given its proper scriptural stress.

James 1:2-4 is a summary of the scriptural view

of Christian character development. It is an inspired expansion of the statement of Paul in Ephesians 2:10, "we are his workmanship." At this point regeneration and sanctification are conceived as a divinely ordained purpose "afore prepared." The most profound thought of which the Christian is capable in committing himself to the will of God is that he is something which God is making. It is significantly accurate that James shows the Master Workman using the crucible of trial to effect the perfect and entire man.

It would be well to examine the complete statement of James's philosophy of Christian maturity. First of all, a man surrounded by a variety of tests is to count it all joy.[1] By faith the Christian is to consider the crucible a place of privilege and great value. Such faith will be soundly based on *fact*.[2] Since we are God's workmanship we can trust Him with our life—even at its worst. We are to know that patient endurance, a priceless virtue, can be obtained in no other way. This is a Christian virtue, available only to the chosen of God. A hypocrite can never attain it. The reprobate may only imitate it.

The actual term which James used in this context does not find its way into many of our translations. It is not the *proving* of the faith which ultimately produces patient endurance. There are many occasions when this is not so. The word which is rendered "proving" in some versions is a neuter term (to dokimion). Thus it should be rendered "that which is genuine."[3] This term is modified by two Greek genitives, "of the faith of you." Thus it means that which is genuine or true in our faith toward God. Granted that James meant what he said, it is the genuineness of our faith which ultimately produces the patience. As the tests of life discover us to be genuine in our faith toward God, God can make us what He desires us to be. If the tests which come to us prove our faith to be counterfeit we abandon ourselves to wisdom that is earthly, sensual, and devilish.

The inspired writer continues this spartan philosophy with an urgent call to submission, "let patience have her perfect work" in order that God may achieve His redemptive objective in you. It is here that God's objective and ours may clash. We piously endorse God's ends but not His means to His ends. The sincerity of the desire to be spiritual will be tested by a willingness to embrace God's way. Is God's heritage in us to be achieved by His means or by our own? This is the cradle of the double mind.

Verse five of chapter one begins with a conjunction of contrast. This contrast is made between God's redemptive objective, "perfect and entire, wanting nothing," and the frank admission of the individual of his obvious lack of moral stability and ethical maturity. He is ready to admit because of his lack that life has found him out. The test has shown him what he is *not*. James offers the solution to this emergency in which all of us find ourselves at one time or another. The escape is found in the nature of the giving God whom man approaches in his need. James points to an impartial God who gives to *all* with liberality. An alternate translation would assure the seeker that God imparts with simplicity.[4] It is not the complexity of God's method which baffles the mind. An all-wise God deals with each man on his own level. It is the rugged path of holy obedience demanded by God which causes the seeker to make a complex issue out of that which God makes a matter of simple compliance. Beyond this the suppliant is assured that God does not rail against him for his past failure or the nature of the need that brought him to the mercy seat.

Such simple requirements as these bring the fulfillment of God's promise, "it shall be given him." However, it is here in the development of the pattern of his thought that James turns the issue inward.[5] The lion detects his prey and roars against the hypocritical act of devotion which ignores the nature and purpose of God. Faith must be a wholehearted, single-souled response to God. The entire person must embrace God *as He is*. If God should show His hand in chastening, are we to doubt His love? If He rebukes us for unbelief are we to question His mercy? Inward concession that God has made His finest contribution to his moral development in adversity carries a man upward in positive spiritual maturity. But mental consent to a principle of Christianity does not suffice. The lack of wisdom can only be supplied by single-minded commitment to the divine direction. It is no accident that great portions of the New Testament are addressed to the believer through the channel of his *will*. Unless the vehicle of language has lost its logic and purpose this implies that a redemptive God moves us in His direction as we move in that direction with Him.

---

1. James 1:2.
2. James 1:3. "Knowing this. . ."
3. Were the intention of James to call attention to the *act* of the proving of our faith he would have used the articular infinitive. By using the neuter idea he calls attention sharply that it is the *genuineness* of the faith of the tested one.
4. The word is *haplos* and may be translated "liberally," as it should be in the Romans 12:8 context of stewardship. The word as used by James is employed in its most persistent usage, *simplicity*, as over against *diplous*, meaning double. There is no need to abandon the idea of more than one meaning in the implication of a word but the idea of simplicity fits the context better here.
5. The mild adversative *de* relates the two expressions as suggested.

6

Friend of the World

Whosoever therefore would be a friend of the world is the enemy of God.
—James 4:4

Opinions on human behavior are probably as old as the art of writing. Generalized statements concerning the characteristics and conduct of men are to be found in the records of all literate people. Even the illiterate have passed on proverbs. The philosopher Plato was at least practical. He insisted that men behave as they do because they have been taught so to behave. This is the academic way of saying, "monkey see, monkey do." The question which this theory raises is where the first man learned to behave. Aristotle, Plato's famous disciple, went beyond his teacher in declaring that the cause for human behavior lay in the nature of the individual. He took the gloomy position that since human nature is unchangeable, society is doomed to remain as it is. Socrates, the father of hedonism, with shrewd analysis of human motive, made it clear that men naturally do that which pleases them and avoid that which displeases them. The thinkers of Rome took a more positive point of view and taught that governmental pressures of reward and punishment can educate human action. This legalistic view is the basis for government to this hour. Other theories ranging from scheming Machiavellism to the novel climate theory of Montesquieu have been propounded to explain man's strange and persistent proneness to adjust to certain patterns of conduct. Modern thinkers attempt to deify the human mind, teaching that as man discovers adequate facts and properly catalogs them in his mind, his conduct will grow safely out of the integration of this logic. By this means he hopes to solve the problems of the world. However, the radical disorder of contemporary life would seem to indicate that experience is not always the best teacher. Man is way ahead with the results of his research which lead to human misery and destruction, but inexcusably slow in ways and means to produce peace. Even his latest medical masterpiece, tranquilizing drugs, for which the American public is spending millions annually, is evidence of the fact that man tends to use his genius to provide a human sedative for the ills of society rather than to seek the divine solution for the problem.

It takes a great measure of intellectual crucifixion to reduce one's thinking to that of a first century psychologist. It can only be done by realizing that James's analysis of human behavior is God's point of view, inspired by the Holy Spirit. No current psychologist has come so simply and forcefully to the point. Chapter four of this epistle, verses one to four, introduces the reader to a line of revealed reason that is unparalleled in human literature as an expose' of human behavior. It begins with one of those disarming questions based on apparent observation of fact. "Whence come wars and fightings among you?" This rhetorical question is followed by the answer, "come they not hence even of your lusts that war in your members?" Although not as thoroughly developed as the moral conflict of Romans seven, it lacks nothing in becoming the simple answer to man's inward need. The problem is *personal, individual, inward, moral.*

As has been stated, the double mind is a condition impossible to any but the child of God. God's child has been made aware of the nature of the problem by the revelation of truth. Bear in mind that the double-minded man is a praying man, a worshiper of God. He is seeking after wisdom from God. There would naturally be no division inwardly if a man were all for self and the world, satisfied with earthly wisdom, sensual conduct, and devilish motivation. Nor would there be any division if a man were all for God, wholly governed by that wisdom which comes down from above. There is no question that the former type of individual exists on every hand. It is to be doubted that such an individual as the latter lives consistently in a state of unquestioned perfection. The problem is to bring the individual to the place where he is willing to admit that all too frequently *both minds* exist within him, marring God's workmanship.

Modern schools of psychology have isolated and given terms to behavior such as James calls to the attention of his brethren in 4:2. Strong desire has been *frustrated* and leads to unseemly conduct. They lust and have not; they covet and cannot obtain, therefore they kill, they fight, they war. This carnal necessity for *compensation* is indicative of moral bankruptcy. It is only a step in the development of James's logic to attribute this barrenness to prayerlessness. "Ye have not because ye ask not." Although James grants that they are going through the *form* of prayer, he goes on to teach them that petition addressed to a giving God with ulterior motives and human objectives is not prayer at all. Because of the holy and changeless nature of God, He remains silent and unmoved at selfish petition no matter how piously worded or fervently uttered. It is not that God is reluctant to give but His impartation is always in harmony with His own nature and His redemptive objective in the suppliant.

It may shock the reader to learn that such an attitude in prayer on the part of the child of God is James's definition of worldliness.[1] In an age of disproportionate negativism masquerading under the misnomer of spirituality, it is purging to our viewpoint to discover that worldliness, enmity to God, is nothing more or less than resorting to earthly, sensual, and devilish religious procedure rather than seeking after and waiting for God's course of action in our lives. Like modern Jacobs the tendency in many of us is to connive for our heavenly heritage rather than to trust God to work in us to will and to do His good pleasure.

This duplicity of character is the basis for James's indignant outcry against the mother church in 3:16.[2] He directs it not so much against the conflict itself as against the heart condition which causes the conflict. Since redemption deals with human character the only seal of its validity is the behavior which it effects in the redeemed. Carnal attempts to bring to pass the blessings of redemption only demonstrate that one has a perverted concept of the nature of God and His objectives. Such wanton disregard of these constitutes spiritual adultery far more tragic than that which Hosea confronted in ancient Israel because it is more enlightened. Now that Israel's Messiah has come and God has given to His people His Spirit to indwell them, such actions as James decries are incongruous, and worse, they are evil.

While the laws of God are set against the use of a worldly set of rules, they fight for the man who single-mindedly adopts those of God's own choosing. It is God's intention that the man submit himself and humbly draw nigh to Him, resisting the devil, cleansing his hands, purifying his double-minded heart. In short, solving the problem of the double mind will amount to a thorough upheaval caused by the brooding of the Spirit over the chaotic waters of the inner man. This is what the old school called revival!

---

1. James 4:4. Thus with James, worldliness is more than a way of life lived around a list of negatives. A person can refrain from every practice which his particular church frowns upon and still be worldly on the ground of this viewpoint.
2. One translation renders it, "...where jealousy and faction are, there is confusion and every vile deed."

7

The Quiet Man

And Jacob was a [quiet] man. . .
        —Genesis 25:27, ASV

Since Scripture is its own best commentary, consider a classic example of the double-minded man—Jacob. The Genesis account subtly describes him as being a quiet man.[1] The Hebrew word suggests that he preferred the quietness of home life to the adventure of the hunt which Esau enjoyed. This preference doubtless afforded him many hours spent in meditating courses of action which make him the foremost historical example of the double mind. His name, Jacob, literally "heel holder," seems to have been prophetic of a disposition which keenly delighted in outwitting his fellow men. The significant detail of this account would never have been recorded had not this man been the chosen of God. It would be unfair to regard it as strictly narration without bearing in mind that it is also divine revelation. What an extraordinary record of the redemptive God in pursuit of the single-minded devotion of a vessel of election!

Bear two things in mind:

1. God, sovereign, immutable, in His dealing with men is relentless in His pursuit of His chosen ones. His unhurried and patient love will not be denied regardless of the extreme measures He may have to take.

2. Jacob, carnal and cunning, chosen of God, has appraised the value of being one of the holy seed and sees in it the touchstone of material and social success. It is true that God will bless him for his father's sake yet such knowledge was to Jacob morally corrupting.

The Church of today is grinding itself to a state of spiritual impotence because men in its ranks are failing to preach and practice that positional righteousness implies practical, personal purity. Like Jacob, the Church needs an encounter with God to convince her that God is interested more in her purity than in her material prosperity. Let it be forcefully stated. All the gifts of the holy, immutable God are granted for *one purpose*—to achieve His redemptive objectives in the moral character of the Christian. Christ Himself said: "Seek ye first the kingdom of God, and His righteousness; and all these *things* shall be added unto you." The most serious indictment that the Husbandman can bring against His vineyard is to place in its midst the winepress of expectancy and find no fruit on the branches (Isa. 5:1-7). This was the moral cause of Israel's exile,[2] of Judah's destruction in A.D. 70,[3] and will be the cause for the denunciation of the unfaithful in our age.[4] Saints without sainthood are a spiritual incongruity which cannot be tolerated by a holy God. Grace does not bind God in a unilateral contract.[5] Redemptive history has proved that there is no immunity from judgment against barrenness. Paul's indictment against smug Judaism in Romans 2:1-10 should be reread with spiritual discernment. It would be no positive contribution to Jacob's concept of spiritual reality to observe the material prosperity with which God blessed his father Isaac in the days of his youth. It is a trait of childhood to take environment for granted. In Isaac we do not see the colorful personality of his father Abraham nor the cunning and impetuosity of his son Jacob. He was content to receive with gratitude the benevolence of God without giving too much in return. Jacob observed his father, a worshiper of Jehovah, practicing deceitful decorum in his dealings with Abimelech. Such practices are transmissable to children. Whereas Isaac practiced deceit with the stranger, Jacob used it within his own family circle. Most astounding is the fact that we see him using it in the sphere of spiritual things! Here is the principle of the double mind using earthly, sensual, devilish wisdom in an effort to achieve the position which

51

God had decreed and prophetically announced.[6] Thus the Jacob narrative is the account of a man who went blundering on in life leaving a trail of little mean encounters with his fellow men. All the while he was congratulating himself for getting on with God's help and the ingenuity of his scheming mind. Still waters ran deep in this quiet man, but not necessarily pure. There is no deception so demoralizing to the spirit as feeling that God can be counted on to cooperate with a man in his carnal climb to religious success. This is obviously the concept that some of us have of the sanctified life.

What an unsavory display of human depravity is that found in the chosen family shot through with deceit and intrigue, plotting and scheming to outwit one another, with the glorious redemptive promises of God as the stake in their wanton gamble! It had become the peculiar treasure of the mother of Jacob that she should be prophetically aware of the ultimate destiny of her unborn children. God, who had given her the strength to conceive, answered her question as to why the children strove within her.[7] With eventual impatience Rebekah began to exercise deep concern. She was not content with the visible course of affairs. Whether it was spiritual concern for the will of God (and this is doubtful) or carnal concern for the welfare of her favorite son, it led her to deceive her husband and her elder son.[8] It also led her to corrupt her younger son with premeditated and base hypocrisy. The details of the story of their trickery are well known.

True to the promise, the blessing *was* transmitted to the younger son. It granted him material prosperity, social rulership, and divine protection.[9] This was all granted without respect to Jacob's personal merit. How much better to have received this blessing of incomprehensible scope in a spirit of love and integrity than in a context of shameful human passions. To be sure, the covenant was protected by virtue of its ultimate realization in Christ. But it causes one to shudder as he realizes that Jehovah had bound Himself in a promise and an oath to the children of Abraham who had little more discernment of His purpose than the pagans around them. It is to the historic credit of Isaac that the discovery of the deception produced in him a state of physical and moral shock.[10] It is to the shame of Rebekah that it led her deeper into the web of deceit. Under the pretense of concern for the proper marriage for her pet son she plans Jacob's escape from the murderous wrath of the cunning hunter, Esau.[11]

The story shifts now to an act of amazing spiritual ignorance. Isaac undertakes the human ordination of an unsanctified vessel which he bases upon a spiritual heritage carnally misappropriated.[12] The only grounds upon which God could bless Jacob was that the Hope of the ages was in his loins. All this while Jacob was nurturing the false spirit of security from the covenant hope of which he was a physical unit, failing in any way to find moral and ethical dynamic in the faith which had characterized his father Abraham.

There is no question that Jacob was God's man of the hour. The Bethel experience gave him a fresh assurance of God's providential care but very little awareness of the personal holiness and changelessness of God. In a shrewd and carnal bargain which showed the grip of the double mind, Jacob became a tither.[13] However, his pledge was grounded on the hypothesis of prosperity. He wore the terms of his agreement like a talisman around his neck as security for a safe trip back home. The reader should note, however, that God accepts the terms of the vow and accepts them at face value in a later encounter.

There is no indignation to compare with that of the double-minded Jacob who suffered from the fruits of the same clever deceit he had practiced upon others.[14] Jacob met in his uncle Laban as good a wrestler as himself. While Laban kept his nephew a virtual vassal, Jehovah was at work in the heart of His chosen one. He was bringing to bear upon him a set of circumstances from which his genius as a supplanter could not extricate him.

It is true that the escape from Laban was cleverly executed. The contagion of lies and deceit had become the way of life for the Jacobean household. He connived with Leah and Rachel to leave Haran, and further presumed upon the faithfulness of God to make good their escape. God did not forsake him. But is a holy God to wink at the theft of Laban's teraphim and overlook the lie by which Rachel concealed them? Laban was brought to the place where he admitted that Jacob had out-wrestled him but only because the Judge was prejudiced.

The natural question here is, why does God own and bless His child despite his unlovely double-minded acts? It is because He is looking at the ultimate objective of His workmanship in His chosen man in Christ. God will wait until His errant children scheme themselves into a set of circumstances where the ability to scheme out is gone. It is here that the gracious, giving God desires that we turn to Him with a single mind and plead for His deliverance. He then knows that we know that it has come from Him.

---

1. Genesis 25:27. The KJV calls him a plain man. The Standard (1901) Version calls him a "quiet man." The margin makes him a harmless man. The Hebrew favors the idea of quietness.
2. One notable example: Jeremiah 17:1-4.

3. Luke 19:15, 16.
4. Matthew 24:45-51.
5. Titus 2:11, 12.
6. See Genesis 25:23.
7. Ibid.
8. Genesis 27:8, 13.
9. Genesis 27:27-29.
10. Genesis 27:33. Isaac "trembled very exceedingly." The extreme language here indicates the highest state of agitation equivalent to shock.
11. Genesis 27:46.
12. Genesis 28:3-5.
13. Genesis 28:22.
14. See Genesis 29:25. Jacob's indignation goes deeper than disappointment; it is the vexation of a wounded pride.

8

The Feet of His Saints

He will keep the feet of his saints.
— 1 Samuel 2:9

When Jacob stole away from the household of Laban with his family and possessions, it is to be doubted that he thought far enough ahead to anticipate the seriousness of the consequences which his past conduct was to bring about. It is innate in humanity to dream about the future but seldom to dream realistically. At this point Jacob would not have appreciated the philosophy of James, "Count it all joy when ye fall into divers temptations. . . ." He knew little of divine providence in relation to the divine direction because he had been content to chart his own course impervious to the will of God.

Although elective grace is primarily a New Testament doctrine it has its roots in the nature of God. His mercy endures forever. His loving-kindness extends to all generations. Thus the unsavory encounter with Laban was tempered by a dream which warned Laban to exercise care in dealing with this child of the covenant.[1] His just indignation had to spend itself upon the insult of the stolen goods. It was a clever piece of deceit which spared Jacob the necessity of carrying out the death sentence upon the one who had stolen the goods. This sentence would have fallen upon his favorite wife.[2] When Laban failed to discover the stolen teraphim it gave Jacob the upper hand, which advantage he quickly grasped and played to the utmost. But both men are forced to admit that it was the hand of God which had prospered and protected Jacob during the past twenty years. His self-effort and double-minded scheming had not brought him *one thing* which God would not have freely granted him *in His own way*—with simplicity as well as liberality.

It is not the purpose of this book to promote a point of view that God is influenced in His giving by human merit or good conduct. It is rather to show that that which a man molds into his character by his earthly, sensual, devilish conduct is morally tragic to him. God is more eternally interested in the spiritual development of the man than in the external blessings which he delights in bestowing. The lowest comprehension of spirituality is displayed by that man who considers material blessings as Exhibit A, showing that he himself is thus endorsed by God as spiritual.

When God warned Laban to speak neither good nor bad to Jacob, Laban may have interpreted this as protective immunity which he dared not trespass. Jacob looked upon it too casually as an indication of divine favor. Both men had a warped impression of God's intention. He was preserving Jacob in the Abrahamic covenant of redemption. Laban drops from the narrative at this point and returns to Haran. Jacob goes forward into the crucible of God's planning in order that he might be taught the nature of genuine faith which would work in him a princehood in harmony with his divine election. He had to learn that being extremely clever in one's dealings may impress men but it never awakens in them a *hunger after God*. The direction in which God desires to set the feet of His saints always leads to the glorification of His own holiness.

At this point it would be helpful to compare the double-minded objectives of Jacob with the redemptive objectives of God and to do so against the backdrop of God's immutable character. Jacob's forthcoming encounter with Esau would call for more than human cunning. Up to this time his application of earthly, sensual, and devilish wisdom had provided a way of escape from every emergency. It had at the *same time* made of him a morally unattractive person. The time had come for God to show *Himself* to His servant.

1. Esau's approach with a small army put Jacob into a state of fear and distress. He thought

only of escape. Escape to him was the basic answer to all crises. It had heretofore always worked. But the philosophy of escape is contrary to the method which God has ordained to make man His workmanship.[3] There are times when God intends for His child to fall into the crucible and "to reckon it joy." It is His means of producing moral character rather than self-congratulation; personal holiness rather than expert strategy.

2. Jacob's approach to God was the bargain-counter type which proved his knowledge of the nature of God was limited. The threat of the approaching meeting with Esau drove him to God. There he is discovered to be a double-minded man, wavering like a wave of the sea driven with the wind and tossed. While it is commendable that he admitted his unworthiness, his appraisal of himself was made in a high state of fear. It is surprising how frankly honest one can be with oneself when *frightened* and how quickly he can get over his fear and forget the unpleasant self-appraisal! God does not want scared saints who vow under pressure to do *better*; He wants strong-hearted godly people who find in Him the ability to do *good*. Jacob wanted escape; God wanted Jacob. Jacob held God to His covenant promises[4] but Jacob was now to discover the God of the covenant.

3. In his double-minded instability Jacob

stooped to bribery. To use his own words, "I will *appease* him with the present that goeth before me, and afterward I will see his face; peradventure he will accept of me." But the policy of appeasement is not better religion than it is politics. It may purchase time and temporary favor but it is character-destroying. God wanted Jacob to learn as Abraham had learned, to "walk before me and be perfect." Jacob's gift could never obliterate his rank injustice to Esau. That was a matter of the heart. Here is the very genius of the Cross, a Pentecost. God made provision for the transformation of spiritual and moral character. To substitute the flimsy veneer of appeasement for the hardwood of remission is, at the least, tyranny against heaven, a tyranny which invites the traditional judgment of a Holy God whose immutable character demands infinite justice.

The reckoning at Penial is not so important as its outcome. Jacob found himself in the grip of the sovereign Wrestler who wanted to bless him in far greater measure than mere deliverance from the wrath of an irate brother. He was now in the skilled hands of the immutable, holy, Giver of good and perfect gifts. As Jacob confessed to the moral disease implicit in his name, supplanter, wrestler, he found God to be a God of transformation as well as provision. A revelation such as this is the gateway to moral and ethical stability.

The very fact that God granted to His servant a new name indicates that he was a different man. There would be no point in changing it otherwise. The change amounted to a new apprehension of the One with whom he had to do. And, it may be added, it was presumptive of Jacob to ask the name of the One with whom he had wrestled through the night. The blessing He imparts can only come from the Giver of every good and perfect gift. Jacob may not have lived up to the spiritual implication of his new name but he could never lapse back into a pre-Peniel attitude toward his God. Once a man has met God as a giver of inward glory (II Cor. 3:18) he can never again regard Him as a mere material convenience. Moral excellence comes at a high price to the flesh, but possessing it in any measure, large or small, as a spiritual impartation from above, gives a bent to the soul which keeps the feet of a saint unhappy and uncomfortable with all else but the divine direction.

---

1. Genesis 31:24.
2. Genesis 31:33-35.
3. Escape is not deliverance. God permits us to fall into various tests that we may know Him better by virtue of His deliverances. Escape is human endeavor to avert that which God desires us to face.
4. Genesis 32:12.

9

The Silent God

For let not that man think that
he shall receive anything of
the Lord.

—James 1:7

It has been established that God has set specific
objectives for men in Christ. He desires that the
Christian shall be perfect and entire; that he shall
love *Him*; that he shall be a special fruit of His
husbandry. James sets forth these objectives
without obscurity or vagueness in his keynote
passage (1:1-18). He refuses to let his beloved
brethren hide behind the flimsy curtain of self-
deception (1:16). The Father of Lights is the only
Giver of good and the Giver of only that which is
good.[1] He desires that His people in every age shall
reflect moral excellence in all their ways, a practical devotion expressed from a heart that is
single-minded in love for Him. It amounts to a
total inward response to that which God has
revealed in His Word as being best for the man.
However, before he can lay hold upon that for
which he has been laid hold upon by God he must
willingly, or by the coercion of divinely appointed
circumstances (as in the case of Jacob or Jonah)

admit his lack. It seems with most of us that the latter principle of coercion is most appropriate. James does not malign his brethren for not being perfect and entire. That is the procedure of the ignorant. It seems pointless for a minister of the Word to harangue his people for worldly and carnal delinquency—a condition of which the honest are already painfully aware. What is needed is a straightforward scriptural plan for deliverance. Denunciation *in itself* is not the remedy for recalcitrant religion. If a man be in Christ, the only solution, as he admits his lack, is in the divine wisdom which God has promised. But if the pull of the world conflicts with the reach after God, such double desires must be resolved in God's favor before He will grant this wisdom.

Conflict such as this may call for soul desperation before the will of God is realized in single-mindedness. Herein lies the necessity for the crucible of testing. What a commentary on the obstinacy of human nature and the long-suffering of God who yearns for our undivided love! James's most vehement denunciations are reserved for the man who does not subject himself to God, cleanse his hands, resist the devil, and purify his double-minded heart (4:7-10).

Thus the frank admission of lack is the first step toward a solution. It is the manner in which wisdom is sought, the sincerity of desire with which it is sought, the willingness of the man to receive it despite the form it takes, the uncomplaining and unquestioning trust in the goodness of the God who grants it, which are imperative. God grants without partiality. He grants with directness and simplicity. He does not mar the eternal beauty of His benediction upon His beloved by upbraiding him for his admitted lack. It cannot be too strongly emphasized or too frequently stated that if the lack should persist the fault does not lie with the gracious Giver but in the seeker himself (1:13, 14).

The expression "praying in faith" has become so trite that it has virtually lost its meaning. Observe that James is asking for a practical manifestation of the faith which a man professes (1:6). He regards the Christian life as an external expression of the inward relation to God through the indwelling Spirit. It may be historically observed that the form and ritual of religion can be *learned*. But inwardness toward God, single-minded devotion, can never be imitated. It can only be *expressed*. Faith is looked upon by James as that conditioner of the entire man which becomes the controlling element of his whole religious expression. Therefore God permits the testing of man to reveal to him whether or not his faith is genuine. Without this faith religion is a vanity (1:26, 27), charity is a mockery (2:15-17), prayer is a travesty without it the religious man lacks stability in maintaining the quality of holy soundness called "wisdom." Thus faith as employed by James is that gaze of the soul which finds a wholehearted concurrence with God in doing what He desires to do in the making of a perfect and entire person. In other words, it is *commitment*.

It is in this context that James presents the silent God. When a man would serve two masters—on the one hand presuming to seek God for wisdom and on the other uncertain that he is willing to pay the price for moral excellence—he commits two evils. He insults the benevolence of a holy and immutable God and regards God's workmanship as being a man with two minds—a *dipsuchos*, as the Greek puts it—professing to be one thing and *doing* another. An immutable God cannot conform Himself to our mundane level or reduce Himself to our earthly ideas. He simply remains silent until the crush of life brings us in desperation to seek Him with a whole heart with faith in His benevolent purpose. The Christian walk is not quiescent meekness which is content to leave everything to God without any effort to channel the mind, the will, and the emotions into the current of the divine direction. The Christian walk is rather the result of faith and faith is the assurance that God *is* and that He *becomes* the "rewarder of them that diligently seek Him."[2] The benevolence and the kindness of God are set forth in such uncompromising clarity and granted with such gracious tenderness that hesitation on the part of the seeker is a betrayal of the "carnal mind which is enmity against God." Such wavering to James is evidence that he does not really desire the thing that he is professedly seeking.

The very fact that God expends His husbandry upon man is ample evidence that man is capable of becoming what God has decreed him to be. Christians are too carnally anxious to resign themselves to the insignificance of their human weaknesses—too contented with little living. James contends that a man can marshal the forces of his own nature and enter the battle for God. God is for man, not against him. Man left to his own resources is a helpless creature but with the ethical energy of God to empower him there seems to be no limit to his spiritual development. So empowered, he is not apt to lose sight of the blessedness of the crown or the sheer joy of divine approval in the grueling demands of God-ordained tests.

A complainer is therefore guilty of pitting his judgments against God's.[3] When a man comes to God for wisdom he must bear in mind that to do so is actively to promote judgment upon his fleshly desires. To grant as did David (Ps. 51:4) that God is just in His judgment against our sin is to open the way for a thorough cleansing. Although David conceded to his human frailty he also recognized that "truth in the inward parts" was the key to wisdom. The mental, volitional, and emotional attitude of the seeker will always be challenged while he is seeking. He must as Elijah be really praying while he prays (*proseuchē proseuxato*)[4] and a man is not really praying unless he fervently desires the thing for which he prays. Here the double mind will show him to be the hypocrite he is. Even as a man prays for the thing he knows he ought to piously desire, his miserable carnality cries out against his prayer being answered.

Unbelief, therefore, with James is not so much doubting that God will answer as a willingness to continue with things going on as they are. Can a man find wholehearted concurrence in the will of God when he has committed himself to finding his greatest joy in the material benefits of this age which God has decreed shall all pass away? Consider rather the logic of Peter: "Seeing then that all these things shall be dissolved, what manner of persons ought ye to be in all holy [living] and godliness. . ." (II Pet. 3:11).

It is the mutual exclusiveness of the Kingdom of God and the kingdom of this world which demands that a man give wholehearted allegiance to one or the other. The double-minded man faces the incongruity of bowing in prayer before a silent God. Moral instability has become with many

Christians not only an occasional display of inward indecision but, as with Jacob, a fixed manner of life which shows an insufficiency of inward steadfastness as well as a woeful ignorance of the character of God. James exhorts his brethren and us to a stability which will cause men to know that we have wrestled with the Angel of God and He has conquered.

---

1. The original contrasts *dosis agathe* with *dorema teleion*. The former qualifies the act of God's giving as being good; the latter the perfection or completeness of the gift.
2. This quotation, Hebrews 11:6, points up faith not only as an assurance of God's existence (the demons have this, Jas. 2:19), but of His nature as a benevolent God, *misthapodores ginetai* (literally, a reward-giver He becomes). Faith consummated is the gift received.
3. James 1:13.
4. James 5:17.

10

The Validity of Virtue

By works was faith made perfect.
            —James 2:22

In the Epistle to the Romans Paul states that the judgment of God will be meted out according to a man's works (Rom. 2:6). James states that Abraham was justified by his works (2:21). These statements are not in the least incongruous with the eternal decrees of God. Let it be noted without any attempt at profundity or innovation that there are works which are the products of man's self-effort. Anything conceived by man or initiated by man through the channel of his own resources can never impart redemptive righteousness in the sight of God. But there are also works which God has eternally ordained for redeemed men to perform (Eph. 2:10) which are conceived by Him, initiated by Him in Christ, and executed by the Holy Spirit. Without them man has no evidence of grace. The judgments of a holy God will be based upon a man's moral character and acts. Thus the cause for judgment is accumulative (Rom. 2:5). Life becomes for the Christian a spiritual investment. At the judgment a man will be the sum total of what he has done by the Spirit. It is readily conceded that we stand justified and at peace with God through Jesus Christ our Lord. If God justifies us no *man* can condemn us. But if God has provided for sanctification of one's life in the Person and power of the risen Christ, then God Himself will hold a man responsible for neglecting it. The entire world then can justly condemn the man who dares profess to be justified without manifesting this sanctifying grace. It is impossible biblically to create a cleavage between a man's character in Christ positionally and his deeds in Christ practically. Yet our insane age of the Church has to a large extent succeeded in creating and foisting such an impression upon her members.

When James maintains that the activity of faith proves the existence of faith, he is saying that Christ's presence *in* a man must be evidenced by Christian virtues in the life of that man. It is as impossible and illogical for Deity to indwell a man without evidence of His presence as it is for fire to burn in a coal without giving off heat and light. How we have succeeded in fixing a great gulf between genuine faith and the works which are an evidence of such faith is the genius of deluded theologians and laymen but hardly the historic philosophy of Christianity. New Testament Christianity swept as a moral force through pagan empires and produced holy, virtuous men—men who would rather die than betray the moral and ethical teachings of the Lord who bled and died for them. If prayer exposes the double mind in its quest for wisdom, certainly vain religion exposes the double mind in its walk before men.

It was not James's intention to face his brethren with further emphasis on doctrinal issues upon which they might exercise their highly developed powers of rationalization and casuistry. In this respect he would be good for our age. The question of the nature of justification by faith would bring spirited discussion with little salutary result. These Jews were well satisfied that they had a saving faith. It is therefore significant that James was led by the Holy Spirit to face them with the fact that the faith which they professed to have was not saving them from themselves. It is here that we who are saved by grace must follow him to his logical conclusion. Neither is the faith which we profess producing the kind of fruit which attests itself to be the product of that wisdom which comes down from above. God has through the ages shown His disgust and contempt for the fruitless. Nothing brought down more wrathful judgment than barrenness under the Old Covenant, and not one line of Scripture teaches that God has deviated from that standard under the New Covenant.

Just what were the traits of Judaism which brought forth the roar from this lion, James? The very nature of the Jew was a puzzling paradox. In spite of a militant monotheism the Jew manifested an insatiable hankering for the world (4:13, 14). His was a peculiar admixture of self-righteousness and pride manifested in careful genealogies. But he was so strongly prejudiced in his religious bent that his zeal was tantamount to a stagnation and crystallization which would not tolerate interference even from the Incarnate God.[1] Yet God Himself had separated this people (Exod. 19:6) to be a kingdom of priests, and a holy nation. This in a particular sense made them a priest-nation with all the nations of the world as their congregation. From the beginning they had been exhorted to singleness of heart. They had been organized for ethical, moral, and social isolation from the world. Moses repeatedly recalled these facts to their memory. They were to love God with the whole soul (*en holē tē psuchē*, Deut. 6:5, LXX). How can those sunken in the slough of self-righteousness be the disseminators of God's redemptive purpose in either word or deed? This is the spirit of Isaiah's message from God to His people; "this people have removed their hearts far from me." On the very brink of the exile Hosea calls attention to their overflowing worldliness and accuses them of a divided heart (Hos. 10:2).

While suffering the judgment of God in the land of exile Ezekiel cried out against their lack of repentance, ". . .for with their mouth they shew much love, but their heart goeth after their covetousness" (Ezek. 33:31). Israel behaved as though she were unaware that her unseemly conduct bore any relation to the nature of the God she professed to worship. Thus God's name was blasphemed among the nations (Ezek. 36:20, 21; cf. Rom. 2:24). Therefore the beloved brethren of James with all their obvious inconsistencies had so perverted their religious sensibilities that God's elective purpose had been obscured in them. Their vain religion (and ours) may be summarized as follows:

1. A complacent trust in a covenant relationship to God expressed physically in the rite of circumcision—*moral stagnation*.

2. An overwillingness to judge that which did not fit the smug pattern of religious dogma—*intolerance*.

3. A miscomprehension of the true character of the God whose Name Israel so jealously guarded—*worldliness*.

Although Israel's zeal rose to heights of heroic patriotism her spiritual effectiveness was ruined by the badge of what we might well describe as a sterile type of fundamentalism.[2] She choked the life out of her religion by setting up a negative theology of the flesh in which a virtue could be claimed without being expressed. This is the masterpiece of the double mind, the workmanship of the flesh. It is sufficient to remark that apostate Judaism and current religion have a great deal in common at this point. A man could *say* he had religion but his unbridled tongue spoke more eloquently than his pious testimony. A man could *say* he had faith but his compassionless heart belied his word to the hungry and naked. A man could *say* that he loved God but his feverish activity in accumulating treasures of this world would show the falsity of his claim. What a perfect picture of the monotonous repetition of history! We possess all the outward trappings of devotion and profess the virtues which flow from the provision of the Cross but our sterility and barrenness have found us out. A generation dies spiritually when its people deny the validity of virtue. A virtue to be valid must be expressed not in word but in deed. "Faith without works is dead."

With James, the crusader for the righteousness of God, there were three alternatives: (1) Single-minded conformity to the redemptive objectives of God; (2) honest conflict until the heavenly Wrestler prevailed; (3) personal chaos wherein the carnal mind, God's avowed enemy, wins the battle. Although this lion uttered his roar with the vocabulary of Judaism he makes us face ourselves with a concept of divine authority. Double-mindedness as James exposed it was the inevitable result of Christian revelation as it engaged the stagnant principles of Judaism in mortal combat. But the validity of his principles is timeless and without dispensational limitation.

Man was created "to glorify God and enjoy Him forever." If sin has rendered him incapable of doing *either* then redemption must enable him to do *both*. There is no moral insufficiency or inefficiency in the plan of salvation. There is only inefficiency in man's apprehension of it. Only those whose relation to God becomes the core of their existence can become involved in the spiritual warfare which makes men godly. Local skirmishes with sin in the spirit of negativism may temporarily impress the public that we are religiously militant but a declaration of total war against the world, the flesh, and the devil magnifies the power of the true God. All Egypt was aware of the omnipotence of God when Moses departed with liberated Israel. Moses' warfare with Pharaoh was more than just a deliverance of Israel, it was a revelation to a pagan nation of the glory of Israel's God. When a man is forced by divinely appointed circumstances to look inside himself to discover the dynamic of the Eternal Spirit to whom he has pledged himself for deliverance, then—and only then—will his soul burn with single-minded love and devotion to God, his

Savior.

---

1. See Matthew 13:53-58.
2. The interested reader may consult II Maccabees for the account of Israel's heroic stand against the unreasonable demands of Hellenism (see particularly II Macc. 7).

11

The Just Shall Live

*Abraham believed God. . .the
just shall live by faith.*
        —Romans 4:3; 1:17

When Habakkuk struggled with the problem of harmonizing God's justice with His judgment against Israel, he was given, by the Holy Spirit, a timeless spiritual principle. How could God in justice send the bloodthirsty Chaldeans to pillage the land and slay His people? Were not the Chaldeans far more ripe for judgment than they? God solved Habakkuk's moral dilemma by revealing His purpose for both the Chaldeans and the chosen nation. In answering Habakkuk He also gave us the answer to questions which pertain to His justice as it is related to His redemptive purpose. As long as faith toward God can fill the heart of a righteous man he can live for his God in any moral crisis.

Paul cites this great principle to substantiate his argument to both the Romans and the Galatians in writing his polemic against Judaism.[1] The righteousness which God imputes through Christ is out of (ek) faith and unto (eis) faith. The writer of the Epistle to the Hebrews in exhorting faltering Hebrew Christians uses the same principle by placing emphasis upon the *life* which ought to be manifest in the one who is walking by faith as his fathers walked.[2]

Thus it is apparent in the four New Testament instances where the issue of ritualistic Judaism versus vital Christianity occurs (viz. Romans, Galatians, Hebrews, James), the heart of the problem is the same. These writings involve at least two men, perhaps three. It is amazing that some scholars have been satisfied to create a division of opinion among the authors of these epistles thereby destroying, in effect, the unity of the Scriptures rather than attempting to find a harmony in that which is obviously a truth with two principles involved. It can be understood and readily forgiven when a man of such single and consuming passion as Luther would call the Epistle of James "strawy." He was a warrior who won a mighty battle by maintaining that a man is justified by faith. It is not so easily understood how men today who are reputedly concerned with "rightly dividing the Word of truth" can question the unity of Scriptures by pitting Paul against James (or by ignoring James) in order to promote a view which could lead to moral carelessness.

This writer stands firmly with James "that by works a man is justified, and not only by faith." In doing so there is quiet confidence that Pauline theology is neither strained nor abandoned. It is maintained that the discovery of the point of harmony is not mental jugglery but is sound exegetical procedure.

1. The Word and Its Meaning

The key word "justify" (*dikaiaō*) without any theological coloration and in its simplest form means "to esteem a thing to be right." It has maintained that meaning to the present day. Because of the unlimited variety of things which may be pronounced right or just and the unlimited number of individuals who may indulge in such a pronouncement, the word is versatile. Our concern is scriptural. Jesus Christ used the word in Matthew 11:19 to fend off unreasonable opinionation of Himself and of John the Baptist. The reader may examine for himself the following observations. (1) The justifier in this passage is an abstract principle—works; (2) the thing justified is wisdom, also an abstract; (3) the justification is the pronouncement that wisdom has acted as she ought to by virtue of the works she performs. Therefore, "wisdom is justified of her children." Without any theological connotation the word here adopts its basic meaning, that of esteeming a thing to be right.

Paul himself uses the word in Romans without any reference to his great theme of justification by faith, in quoting from Psalm 51:4 to support a statement concerning God's justice. The reader may examine it for himself in Romans 3:4 to note the following facts: (1) The justifier here is David; (2) the One who is justified is *God*; (3) the justification has to do with the nature and intensity of the judgment which David is to suffer because of his great sin. Whatever God would demand in justice against David would be esteemed right as far as David was concerned.

Another instance which ought to settle this point is to be found in Luke 10:29.[3] Note the following: (1) The justifier and the justified are the *same* person: (2) the justification is the desire of the individual to esteem *himself* right in his point of view in the eyes of Jesus.

These instances serve as convincing proof that Paul used the word in a sense different from the one in which James used it if (1) the thing esteemed to be right were different (2) and the one esteeming it to be right were different. Let's look at the facts.

2. The Point of Reference

The two writers are discussing *different events* in the life of Abraham. Paul in his great chapter concerning Abraham's faith (Rom. 4) begins by making reference to Genesis 15. Abraham has asked God for an heir. God has assured Abraham that he shall have an heir who shall be his own flesh and blood (15:4). At this divine declaration that he shall be a *father*, Abraham's heart believes God's promise. God seeing his heart response "reckoned it to him for righteousness." Paul is here referring to *one thing only*—the fact that God saw his heart response, esteemed it a *right response* and graciously reckoned it unto him for righteousness.

James in his great dissertation on works (2:14-26) is referring to another incident (v. 21)—the offering up of Isaac upon the altar. The Genesis account (chapter 22) shows that God's purpose was clearly to *prove* Abraham. The crux of the matter comes in Genesis 22:18 where God places the emphasis upon Abraham's *obedience*—"because thou hast obeyed my voice." Any reasonable examination of the facts will show that Paul is concerned with the *faith* of Abraham in the *promise* of God; James is concerned with the *obedience* of Abraham to the command of God.

3. Contextual Considerations

Paul and James are writing of different issues. Romans is a redemptive polemic and thus may be described as an open battle against Judaistic legalism. James is an ethical and practical epistle written to Jews. Paul cites Abraham as an example of one who had a faith unto justification. He is showing that the Old Testament record of both David and Abraham proves that faith (not law) was the justifying principle. Paul is discussing a heart attitude toward God, a steadfast acceptance of God's promise. It should be borne in mind that God was the only One capable of pronouncing Abraham's heart condition as right in His sight. It was an attitude known by God alone, and *God alone* pronounced him righteous. The issue with Paul is not so much the acts of Abraham or even his ethical character. It may be noted in harmony with the theme of this book that Abraham lapsed into double-mindedness in his impatience to bring to pass by fleshly activity that which God had promised supernaturally. But at the point where Paul calls attention to the record, a gracious God is looking upon a single-minded response in the heart of His child. His good pleasure in what He saw was evidenced by the fact that He pronounced it righteousness. Paul then is engaged in contrasting faith with unbelief.

With James we are brought face to face with another matter. The child Isaac has been born according to the promise. The doting father has made an idol of this son of his old age. Now *obedience* will be the test of *faith*. There is a faith of orthodoxy and there is a faith of orthopraxy![4] Without the latter the former is vain. A barren faith is no faith!

To translate the principles adopted by the two writers into current terminology, Paul is saying: "Works cannot give you a right standing before God; He sees your heart response to His Word." James is saying: "The kind of faith that gives assent to God and His Word and does nothing about it is not faith at all." Paul is concerned with God *esteeming a man* right inwardly because of his faith in the finished work of His Son. James is concerned with *man esteeming himself* in right standing with God inwardly when his outward conduct bears witness to his inward barrenness.

4. Semantics

The word "justify" is not the only word which James and Paul used with a different implication. James probably wrote his epistle some time before those of the precise and logical Paul. It was Paul who invested words with precise and theological meaning. It might be added that Paul has been aided and abetted by his many interpreters since. With Paul faith is full acceptance of God and His promises. James, however, refers more in the context under discussion to specific statements about God's nature and the attitude which his beloved brethren should manifest in their *conduct* in the light of these statements. Paul refers to *the principle of belief* in God's redemptive acts in Jesus Christ; James refers to *the principle of response* to certain facts about God which ought to make a man conscious of his brother's need. James decries dead works which a man brazenly substitutes for vital Christian living. The works which Paul despises could be produced without any relation to Christ or without any empowerment of the Holy Spirit. One man, Paul, fights against dead legalistic Judaism because he realizes that God has provided life in Christ alone. The other, James, fights against dead legalistic orthodoxy because he realizes that God has provided life in Christ which can be the only motivation of a people sadly devoid of Christian conduct. Paul is concerned with right standing, James with right behavior. Paul makes it clear that the ungodly man can be justified (esteemed right in God's sight) by faith; James makes it clear that only the man who *does right* in God's sight can be justified (esteemed right in making such a claim) in saying he has faith. How can a man *live* by his faith if he is not justified? How can a man be justified if he does not *live* by his faith? Paul and James could find fellowship on this issue after the great Council at Jerusalem.[5] The same fellowship must be found in our thinking today if we would be delivered as justified men from the snare of dead orthodoxy!

---

1. Romans 1:17; Galatians 3:11.
2. Hebrews 10:38.
3. "But he, willing to justify himself, said unto Jesus, And who is my neighbor?"
4. Defined by *Oxford Universal Dictionary* as "righteousness of action; practical righteousness."
5. Galatians 2:9.

12

A Hedge about Him

*Hast thou not made an hedge
about him, and about his
house, and about all that he
hath on every side?*
　　　　　—Job 1:10

History has proved that Satan is a better theologian than many professors of theology. It should be soberly admitted that he operates in our day as he did in the day of Job. There are in Job two observations to be made which have no dispensational qualifications as to our adversary: (1) Satan was aware of God's protection of His own servant (Job 1:10). (2) Satan was aware that he had to deal with a God whose holy, immutable, and benevolent nature would not be violated in his dealings with Job (1:12; 2:6). The blessing of a benevolent God has always been upon His children but it has always been contingent upon their obedience to Him (Deut. 6:10-15).

James recalls to his brethren this aspect of God's character in 5:11 in an expression—"the *end* of the Lord."[1] God's end, or purpose, in Job (to whom James makes reference) was shown to be in harmony with God's very nature. The pain and raw misery, physical and mental, which Job suffered were for a good purpose and therefore permitted by the Lord who is "full of pity, and merciful." This simple philosophy of suffering has eluded some of us in our learned discussions about God's provision for the physical body. In spite of the stigma which the biblical doctrine of physical healing has carried in our generation, there is no reason to make it a doctrine of embarrassment among those who believe it. Nor is there any good reason to consign it to an apostolic doctrine among those who refuse it. Wild-eyed, publicity conscious, faith healers have given the practice of healing international notoriety. It has gone so far as to deeply disturb European royalty and cause caustic comment in newspapers and magazines. It might even seem in some instances to have become a lucrative "racket" when exploited cleverly. Little wonder that reputable Bible teachers and pastors have been silenced! Nevertheless this truth cannot be explained away in embarrassed haste because it has been abused! It was abused in apostolic days also (Acts 8:9-13). Should we disparage the Philips in the Church because there are Simons on the loose?

On the ground of biblical honesty the true issue becomes one of inspiration and then one of exegesis. If James is canonical then 5:13-18 belongs to the Church. If it belongs to us then we must find out what it tells us and embrace it.

Surprisingly enough it is in the matter of healing that the double mind is most sharply defined by James. In dealing with God in the sphere of the spiritual we are involved in the abstract. In dealing with Him in the physical sphere there can be no deceit. Even Jesus Christ admitted that it was easier to say "thy sins be forgiven thee" than to say "take up thy bed and walk." When a man is healed by the mighty power of a supernatural God he is restored to soundness and there is no question in his mind or anyone's mind who observes it that he is *healed*. There is just as much (or even more) charlatanism in the public approach to sin by the professional logic of "easy believism" as there is in "faith healing." Many a deluded soul has been tricked into a premature "instrument birth" pronouncement of regeneration by an overeager altar worker, only to discover later that the Word which he received "anon with joy" has wilted away by the cares and pleasures of life. There will always be counterfeits in religion as long as there is Christianity (II Tim. 3:5-9). Until we learn to settle our principles upon sound exegesis of the text of the Bible rather than upon sentimental endorsement of denominational declarations we will go on letting the charlatans operate without a serious or effective challenge.

There are some sound and sensible scriptural principles which any Bible believing Christian can accept. James is to be credited for setting them down for us. He conditions his doctrine of healing by them.

1. *The divine direction is preeminently spiritual.* He wrote: "that ye may be perfect and entire"; "promised to them that *love Him*"; "that we should be a kind of firstfruits of His creatures."[2] James has called the attention of his brethren to the "end of the Lord." With Job, as with all of us, God's end in view is always to conform us to the image of His Son. This deceivingly simple fact is sufficient to deter any wise servant of the Lord from placing the use of the doctrine of physical healing in a position above *any* spiritual factor in God's purpose. God's sovereign will for His children is for their spiritual development. Therefore His will for their physical well-being must always be kept *secondary.* It is scripturally substantiated that God uses physical pain and suffering to achieve His spiritual purpose. We cannot, yea *dare not,* set one aspect of God's will against another without being guilty of double-mindedness. Only a double-minded man would seek God for physical well-being to the detriment of his soul. To *feel* better rather than to *be* better is the cry of the flesh. It is certainly not the thirst of the soul!

2. *The human will must always be brought to single-minded acceptance of the will of God.* This

is fully implied in the language of the text. At least three factors are indicative of this:

a. "*Let him call for the elders.*" This word, *proskalesasthō* has a double significance as touching the human will. It is in the imperative mood which is always directed to the will. It is in the middle voice which denotes that the one who calls shall take the initiative in the calling. This is therefore rendered "let him call [for himself] the elders." Need it be said that such a requirement is a virtual impossibility in mass healing campaigns? The public call for candidates for healing generally speaking brings to the "healer" a checkered group of individuals such as those who crowded against the Son of God in the days of His flesh—hedonistic, self-centered, double-minded seekers, many of whom have no higher motive than *escape.*

b. "*Let them pray over him.*" This construction is identical with the above and thus calls for a united session of prayer with a single objective *ep' auton, over him.* This requirement makes more of a demand upon the impotent resources of the local church than can be imagined. It is not so easy to find a group of mature, spiritual, stabilized believers (*presbuterous*) who can unite hearts and wills over a sick brother. If our doctrinal views do not spoil the unity, our dispensational dismissal of the healing prerogative would!

c. *"The prayer of faith. . . ."* This seems the most rigid requirement of all. Interpreted in the light of James 4:2-4 it would seem that inward wars, frustrations, carnal desires, and double-minded attitudes would destroy the faith of the brethren. Especially is this true as we examine the kind of prayer that "availeth much in its working." The praying man must be righteous. It is only the just who *live* by faith. Unforgiven sin may not change our status before God but it certainly destroys our confidence before Him. Thus James calls for confession of sin in the elders (5:16) as well as in the afflicted (5:15). There is no element of cynicism in the following question. Where are we to find a body of elders who will band together with holy desire, willing to confess before each other their accumulated sins, pray for one another until they can with single-minded confidence petition God with boldness for the physical need of an afflicted brother? If such can be found *so can* the deliverance be found! It is always people who have forfeited the simplicity of faith because of their sins who look to their theologians to redefine and adjust their doctrines to their moral level. The revival of genuine Christianity in the Church is always accompanied by a resurgence of her supernatural gifts.

Since Elijah is cited as the illustration of a righteous man who prayed as men ought to pray for the sick, an examination of the facts will be helpful.

Elijah had no special personal virtue. He was a man of like nature and feelings with us. He possessed no "healing angel" and claimed no charismatic ability.

Elijah prayed in the will of God; his prayer was in the name of Jehovah. Let us not envision Elijah as a fanatic freelancer turned loose upon Israel to be governed by his own initiative. Let it be understood that no man commands the heavens to be closed or opened by his own whim or fancy. Neither does any man in our day command God to do anything which He Himself has not already decreed He *will do.* Neither will God waive the conditions under which He has decreed He will do it. Elijah was God's representative in an age of extreme moral crisis. Read the declaration in I Kings 17:1 ff., and it will be seen that the language denotes that he was merely the messenger of God. That *God's* will was performed is substantiated by God's promise of sustenance of His prophet at the brook Cherith in the awful days that followed (I Kings 17:4).

"*It rained not. . .the heavens gave rain.*"

The validity of any procedure is the seal of heaven upon it. God attested to the faith of Elijah's prayer by granting precisely what he prayed. Does it need to be said that in double-mindedness there cannot be the seal of heaven upon the practice of any scriptural prerogative? The representative of the Church can mouth orthodox formulas and peddle pious platitudes with no more serious consequences (or results) than the boredom of the listeners or their effusive dutiful commendation as they leave the sanctuary. It is *impossible* to practice the doctrine of healing with any success unless God's conditions are *met*. Too long have many laid upon the unhealed the charge of "hidden sin" or "lack of faith" rather than face the embarrassment of personal failure to meet God's holy requirements!

When one sensibly and honestly eliminates from the business of "wholesale healing" those individuals with whom a patient God is effecting His spiritual purposes, as well as those who fail to meet His conditions because of stubborn double-mindedness, the facts are not hard to face. When it is admitted that God is silent toward those who do not seek Him with a whole heart then it is not the biblical doctrine of healing that is to be called in question. It is rather those who practice it in *defiance* of the nature of the God who has promised to "save him who is sick" and the faithfulness of the Lord who "shall raise him up." It would be refreshing to see a revival of genuine biblical healing within the boundaries of divine promise which would lay aside the rubbish of humanism and naturalism and embrace the Almighty and giving God with single-minded desire to ask in faith, nothing wavering or doubting. It is the opinion of James the Just under divine inspiration that it would be given to him!

What we call *simplicity* of faith then is nothing more or less than *purity* of heart. We need only "draw nigh to God and He will draw nigh to us. Cleanse your hands, ye sinners; and purify your hearts, ye double minded," is God's final word in every area of Christian experience, the area of divine healing not excepted!

---

1. From *telos* meaning a designated or purposive end.
2. These statements have already been discussed as to their spiritual implication in Chapter 3, "*The Divine Direction.*"